POP·UP
GREETINGS CARDS

POP·UP

GREETINGS CARDS

OVER 50 SIMPLE·TO·MAKE PROJECTS

MIKE PALMER

CHARTWELL
BOOKS, INC.

A QUINTET BOOK

Published by Chartwell Books
A Division of Book Sales, Inc.
110 Enterprise Avenue
Secaucus, New Jersey 07094

This edition produced for sale
in the U.S.A., its territories
and dependencies only.

ISBN 1–55521–897–0

This book was designed and produced by
Quintet Publishing Limited
6 Blundell Street
London N7 9BH

Project Editor: Laura Sandelson
Creative Director: Richard Dewing
Designer: Peter Laws
Editor: Michelle Clark
Illustrator: Tony Townsend
Photographer: Paul Forrester

Typeset in Great Britain by
Central Southern Typesetters, Eastbourne
Manufactured in Singapore by Eray Scan Pte. Ltd.
Printed in Singapore by Star Standard Pte. Ltd.

CONTENTS

INTRODUCTION

ave you ever been sent a pop-up greetings card? If so, you can probably even now remember the design of the card, who sent it and on what occasion. A pop-up card is memorable.

What makes a pop-up card so special? Perhaps it's because a pop-up card is more than just a card – it is a surprising and amusing gift in its own right. What's more, a pop-up card cannot help but draw attention when it is displayed alongside conventional cards, reminding everyone of who sent it and making the receiver feel extra-special (which, after all, is the original aim of sending a card). Indeed, a pop-up card is often kept on display long after conventional cards have been put away.

The pop-up cards in this book have been carefully designed to show a range of interesting techniques, from easy to quite advanced, to appeal to all levels of papercraft and pop-up enthusiasts. Few cards require any drawing ability, though, clearly, the more fluency you have with a pencil, the more options will be available to you. The template drawings, however, give clear guidance to those readers who need help with shapes and sizes.

Pop-up cards need to be made with care and precision. Making them sloppily will only end in frustration, so take your time and *think* your way through each design.

Please read the first chapter, Getting Started, as it contains useful advice on all that you need to know about this straightforward but completely absorbing craft and guides you through the step-by-step procedures common to all pop-up constructions. Skip it at your peril!

I very much hope that this book will inspire you to create your own pop-up designs and that, by doing so, you will enjoy making them and giving them.

MIKE PALMER

GETTING STARTED

10

DECORATION IDEAS

The decoration of a pop-up greetings card is an important aspect of the design and must be approached thoughtfully. In particular, the choice of media is crucial, as the incorrect choice can ruin your construction. So . . .

DON'T

. . . use water-based paints, such as poster paints, gouache or watercolour, on ordinary card as the water will make the card "cockle" – wrinkle and warp. If you must use them, an alternative is to use heavy watercolour or etching paper, which are made to hold water without cockling. Even thick markers will cockle most papers and some thin cards, so take care.

Remember, a pop-up piece that has cockled will not lie flat when the greetings card is closed up, so preventing the card from shutting. Thus, cockling is not only unsightly, but also affects the pop-up mechanism.

DO

. . . use media such as felt pens, coloured pencils and inks (but no washes). Oil pastels, dry pastels and charcoal may be used, but should be well fixed to avoid them transferring when the card is shut flat. Consider also using other decorative techniques, such as stickers, glitter, collage and coloured card. Really, anything is acceptable, so long as it looks good. Remember, though, that too much decoration can distract from the cleverness of your construction and from the three-dimensional shapes that magically appear when the card is opened. Indeed, many pop-up cards look stunning simply left plain!

EQUIPMENT

The list of essential equipment for making pop-up cards is pleasingly simple and short. Most items can be bought inexpensively at most stationers or art and craft suppliers. You will need a:

1 craft knife

2 scalpel

3 metal safety rule or straight edge

4 scissors

5 pencil

6 eraser

7 masking tape

8 glue

9 self-healing cutting mat

12

BASIC TECHNIQUES FOR MAKING POP-UPS

Throughout the book, two simple pop-up techniques recur many times: the "V" fold and "tab" techniques. The construction procedure for both techniques is explained in the following paragraphs and not repeated in each project, so please refer to these pages when they occur in the projects. The procedures for other techniques are explained as they occur.

KEY

⎯⎯⎯ mountain crease
⎯⎯⎯ valley crease

mountain crease

valley crease

"V" FOLD

This is a very simple but wonderfully versatile pop-up technique. The two halves of a pop-up form are glued to the backing sheet so that each half falls each side of a crease, to create the "V" shape. Note the presence of glue tabs at the bottom.

1 This is the basic "V" fold form. The glue tabs fold away from the "V".

2 Apply glue to the undersides of both tabs.

3 Glue one tab to the backing sheet in such a way that the point where the two tabs meet touches the crease on the backing sheet.

4 Fold the other half of the backing sheet over the top of the "V" fold, to glue itself to the upper tab.

1

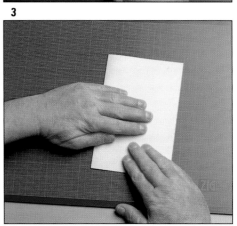

3

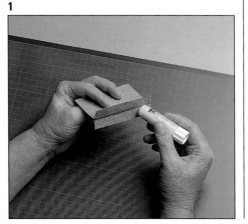

2

4

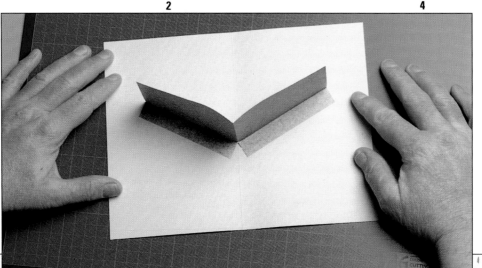

5 Unfold the sheet to see the three-dimensional "V" fold. By following steps 1–4, the "V" fold is guaranteed to lie flat within the pop-up card.

*T*AB

Unlike the "V" fold technique, the tab *must be measured* before being constructed, otherwise it will not collapse within the pop-up card when it is closed. Note that the construction technique is the same whether the tab is a separate piece of card that is glued to the backing sheet in the correctly measured position or whether the tab is cut away from the backing sheet, as explained here.

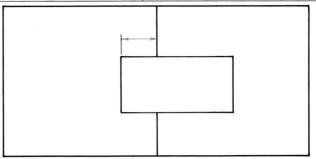

3 Measure AB, the distance between the central crease and the *nearer* end crease, here to the left.

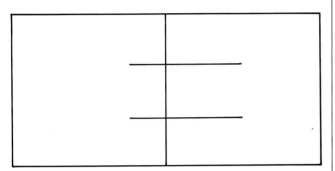

1 Draw the vertical crease on the backing sheet and draw two horizontal cuts (neither crease nor cut yet).

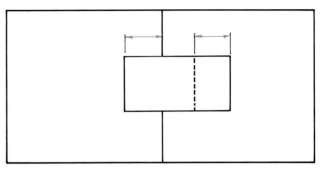

4 Reproduce that distance at the other end. This will locate the position of the mountain crease on the finished pop-up element. Draw in the crease.

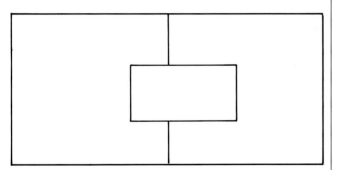

2 Erase the part of the crease between the two cuts. Draw two more vertical creases, parallel to the first (centre) crease.

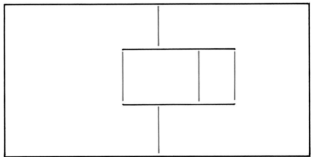

5 Only now, cut and crease your drawing, to create the perfect collapsible tab pop-up mechanism, with all the creases correctly placed.

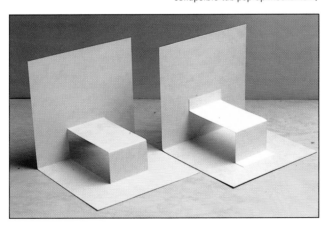

6 The tab pop-up mechanism is complete. Note how in one the tab is glued to the backing sheet, while in the other, the tab is cut from the backing sheet.

14

HOW TO MAKE AN ENVELOPE

The pop-up cards in this book conform to no particular proportions when they are folded flat: some are almost square, whereas others are long and thin. All of this means that few will fit snugly into a standard, bought envelope.

One solution is to re-proportion the backing sheet so that the card *will* fit into a standard envelope, but this can pose tricky measurement problems.

Another solution is to make your own envelope. On these pages, two envelopes are suggested: a practical postal envelope and a decorative presentation envelope.

POSTAL ENVELOPE

This is a version of the classic postal envelope that, carefully made, will securely hold a pop-up card when it is mailed. Use strong, medium-weight paper to make it.

Cut out the shape of the envelope as shown, changing the proportions to suit your card. Pay careful attention to the shapes of the four tabs, making sure that they overlap each other enough to allow adequate gluing. Use strong paper glue.

KEY

——	cut along this line
——	valley crease
▭	glue here (sometimes on the underside)

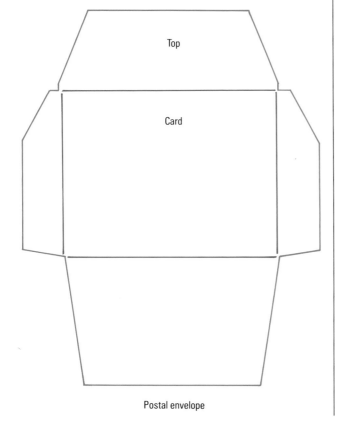

Postal envelope

1 Fold in the side flaps.

2 Fold up the bottom edge.

3 Open the bottom edge and apply glue to the side flaps underneath, where the bottom edge lies on top.

5 Before mailing, apply glue to the top flap to close the envelope.

4 Insert your pop-up card.

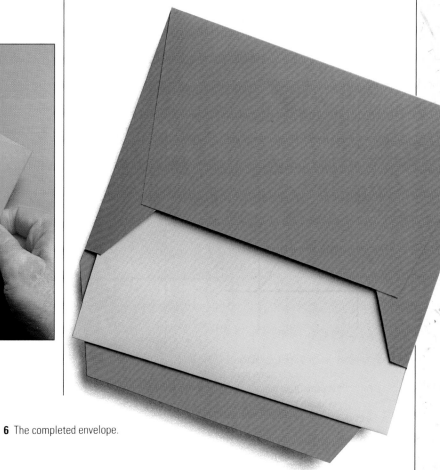

6 The completed envelope.

18

HOW TO CONSTRUCT
YOUR POP-UP CARD

The template drawings and the step-by-step photographic instructions for each pop-up project give most of the information you will need successfully to make up any design in the book. However, although the designs are different, there are certain procedures that are common to all constructions, so here is a point-by-point check list that takes you through them. Please read it carefully and refer back to it when you are constructing particular projects later on.

THE TEMPLATE DRAWINGS

The drawings of the separate pop-up pieces laid out on the template grids are correctly proportioned, one to another, but will need to be enlarged (unless you want to make a miniature pop-up card, of course!). This can be done in one of two ways. You can draw a grid of squares of the appropriate size on a sheet of scrap card, then transfer the template drawings to it following the lines in each square. Alternatively, photocopy the template drawings from the book and enlarge them with further photocopies, then sandwich a sheet of carbon paper between the photocopy and the card and draw over the lines of the photocopy, carefully holding the paper in position as you do so.

The size of the backing sheet of the cards we made is given on the template grid. The dimensions are of the *open* backing sheet (ie not folded in half): the first dimension is of the edges bisected by the crease. In addition, an important measurement of a major pop-up piece is given, to relate its size to that of the backing sheet. The sizes of the other pop-up pieces can be gauged from this measurement. If you want to create a card that is larger or smaller than the one shown, the measurements of the backing sheet and the pop-up pieces must be adjusted *in proportion.*

FIRST, MAKE A ROUGH CARD

It is always tempting to rush straight into making a finished pop-up card, but, unless you are experienced and feel that you fully understand the construction techniques, you are *strongly* advised to *first* make a rough card.

Many people – for some reason – become embarrassed at the thought of making a rough, perhaps because it seems a little childish or as though they have failed before they have begun. However, even professionals begin this way. They recognize that, by solving all the problems

and understanding the inevitable idiosyncrasies of a design before the final version is made, both time and materials are saved.

Your rough can be as rough as you wish – nobody will see it. Make it from scrap paper or card and include only the necessary elements. Practise decoration techniques, too, so you can see what will work and what won't.

MATERIALS

The "Materials" boxes at the head of each project show what materials were used in the step-by-step sequences. However, it must be stressed that these materials *are only a suggestion*. In particular, the weights of paper and card may change from those suggested, according to what is to hand. Remember, though, that as a general rule, the backing sheet should be stiff: if a decorative surface is required, attractive paper or thin card can be glued to stiff mounting card.

The decorating techniques and media (coloured pencils, felt tip pens, etc) are also only a suggestion. You are strongly encouraged to use media of your own choice.

DECORATING THE CARD

When your rough card has been completed, you can then make your finished version. If the pieces of card are to be decorated, the decoration must be done *before* the pop-up elements are assembled. Whether this is done before or after each piece has been cut away from a larger sheet is a matter of personal choice.

GLUING THE CARD

Always use glue sparingly. If it seeps out from beneath a tab, the whole pop-up mechanism will stick together when it is folded shut, spoiling all your careful work.

Never use glues that bond instantly or double-sided sticky tape, as you will probably want to slide the newly glued piece around a little, to enable the card to fold neatly shut. Instead, use a good-quality paper glue, preferably with a nozzle, so that you can direct the flow. Screw-out glues are good, but can be messy.

ASSEMBLING THE CARD

Assemble each greetings card piece by piece, in the order suggested by the text. Work methodically and carefully: pop-up designs are geometric structures that do not work if they are assembled in a haphazard manner. Test each piece for shape and size before gluing it into position.

20

STABILIZING A 90° CARD

When complete, some cards that open up to 90° (instead of opening flat to 180°) have the irritating habit of wanting either to close up or open out more than intended, spoiling the design. To stabilize such a card, it may be necessary to add a wing – to the front (if the card wants to close up) or to the back (if the card wants to open out). These wings can be cut from the backing sheet, or separate pieces may be glued on. For symmetrical stability, two wings may be needed near the left and right edges of the card.

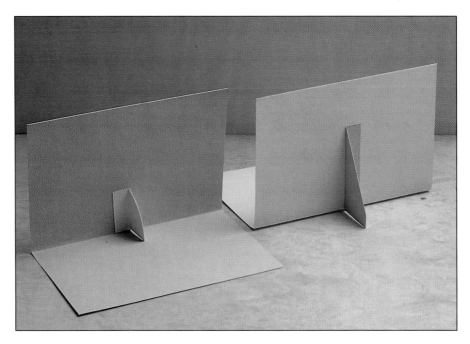

OPENING A 180° CARD COMPLETELY FLAT

A card that is meant to open completely flat will not do so if the crease on the backing sheet is scored (if the card is heavy) or folded by hand (if the card is light). The card must be cut into two halves along the crease, then the pieces joined back together again so that they will lie flat.

CHRISTMAS

OH, TANNENBAUM

This design is simpler to make than the other Christmas Tree card later in this chapter and can be simplified even further if the tub and tree are made from a single piece, but is still incredibly effective. Decorate your tree with lots of colourful, sparkly bits and pieces for a really festive air.

MATERIALS
● backing sheet: thin grey card glued to mounting card
● tree and tub: thin grey card
● felt tip pins

SIZES
backing sheet: 20 × 21 cm/ 8 × 8½ in
height of tree: 20 cm/8 in (excluding tabs)
scale of grid: 1:2

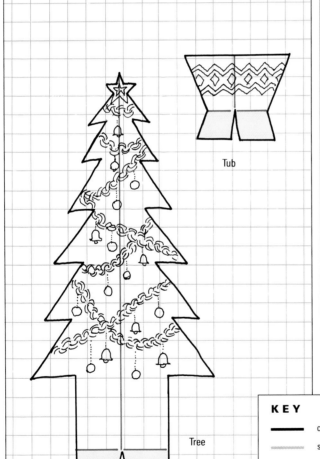

Tub

Tree

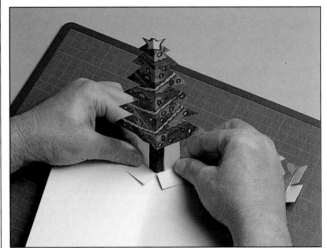

1 Apply glue to the underside of the tree tabs.

2 Glue the tree to the backing sheet, using the "V" fold technique (see Getting Started, earlier).

KEY	
——	cut along this line
∿∿∿	suggested artwork
——	mountain crease
——	valley crease
▭	glue here (sometimes on the underside)

3

Apply glue to the underside of the tub tabs.

5

When the card is shut, the tree and tub will tip forward.

4

Glue the tub to the backing sheet, using the "V" fold technique once more and positioning it a little way in front of the tree trunk.

FOR BEST RESULTS...

- Do not overglue the tabs.
- For a totally flat backing sheet, follow the method described in Getting Started under "V" fold.

24

JOLLY SNOWMAN

✳✳

The pop-up technique used here is the conventional "V" fold, but the strap across the central crease makes the snowman stand to one side, to create an unusual asymmetric variation. If the strap was removed, the snowman could be glued to the central crease.

MATERIALS

- backing sheet: thin textured white card glued to mounting card
- snowman and strap: thin textured white card
- felt tip pens

SIZES

backing sheet: 26 × 15 cm/
10¼ × 6 in
height of snowman: 11 cm/
4½ in (excluding tabs)
scale of grid: 1:2

KEY

— cut along this line

~~~~~~ suggested artwork

━━━ mountain crease

━━━ valley crease

▭ glue here (sometimes on the underside)

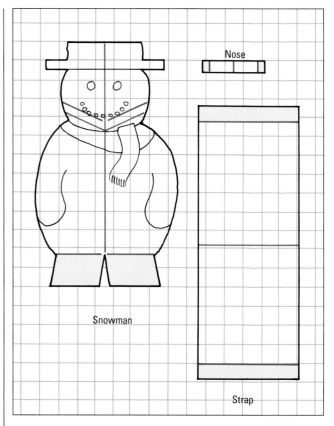

Nose

Snowman

Strap

 Apply glue to both tabs on the strap, then glue it flat across the backing sheet, aligning the central crease on the strap with the crease on the sheet.

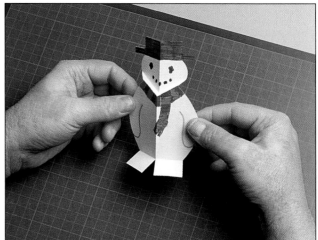

 Create the creases on the snowman's neck.

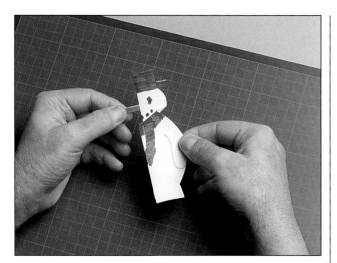

 3 Push the nose tabs through the slit on the head and glue.

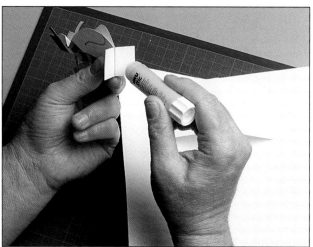

 5 Glue the snowman to the strap, using the "V" fold technique (see Getting Started, earlier).

 4 Apply glue to the underside of the snowman tabs.

FOLLOW YONDER STAR

***

An underused pop-up technique is that of the zigzag crease, which lifts a pop-up shape away from the support that connects it to the backing sheet. The star shown here could be made to pop up without the creases beneath it, but it would not then thrust forward as much as it does, which adds to the impact.

MATERIALS

- backing sheet: thin pink gloss card glued to mounting card
- support: thin pink gloss card
- star: thin silver card

SIZES

backing sheet: 33 × 11 cm/
13¼ × 4½ in
height of star: 10 cm/4 in
scale of grid: 1:2

KEY

———— cut along this line

———— mountain crease

———— valley crease

▭ glue here (sometimes on the underside)

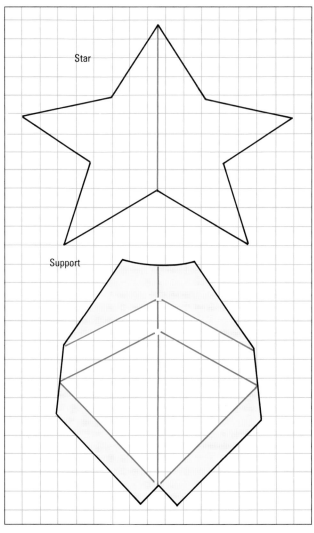

Star

Support

1 *Apply glue to the support, beneath where the star will sit.*

2

Glue the star to the support as follows.

 3 *The edges of the star and support should align.*

4 *Apply glue to the underside of the support tabs.*

 5 *Glue the support to the backing sheet, using the "V" fold technique (see Getting Started, earlier).*

 6 *When the card is folded flat, the star will tip forward and outward, hence the extra width of the backing sheet.*

BE CREATIVE

The creased support that elevates the star need not be the shape suggested here. For example, it could be elongated or widened, perhaps to support a shape other than a star, such as a Birthday name or numeral. Further creases may be added.

FESTIVE FIR

****

The pop-up design here may seem simple, but take care with it as the construction needs to be very precise in order for it to work well. In particular, attention must be paid to how the base of the tree pieces glue to the inside of the tub, as the measurements and creasing need to be accurately done. You will know when you have got it right because the tree will open gracefully.

<table>
<tr><th>MATERIALS</th><th>SIZES</th></tr>
<tr><td>• backing sheet: thin orange card glued to mounting card
• tree and tub: green and brown thick paper</td><td>backing sheet: 36 × 32 cm/ 14½ × 12¾ in
height of tree: 19 cm/7½ in
scale of grid: 1:2.5</td></tr>
</table>

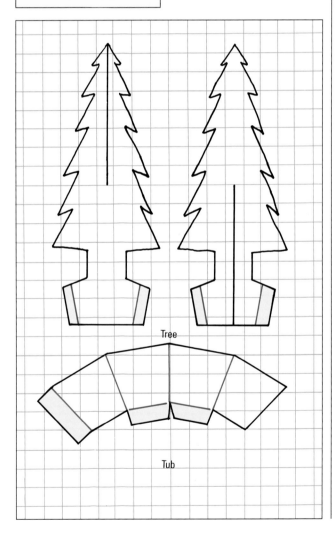

Tree

Tub

1

Note the differently placed slits on the two tree halves.

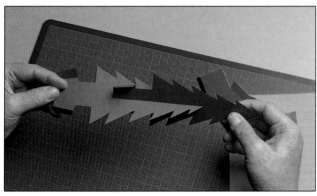

2

Interlock the slits.

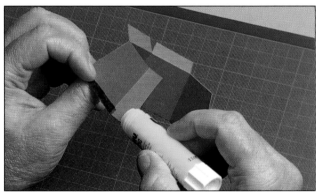

KEY

— cut along this line

— mountain crease

— valley crease

☐ glue here (sometimes on the underside)

3

Apply glue to the end tab on the tub, then form the square tub.

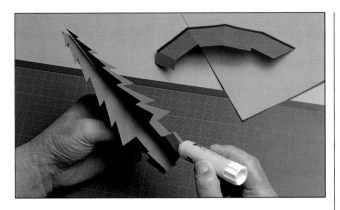

 Apply glue to the four tabs at the base of the tree.

 Apply glue to the underside of the tub tabs, then glue the tabs to the backing sheet using the "V" fold technique (see Getting Started, earlier).

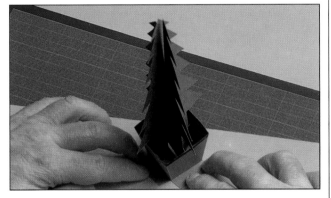

Glue the tree tabs to the inside of the tub so that the crease on each tree tab lies exactly down the centre of each tub face.

 Though very three-dimensional, the tub and tree will easily collapse flat when the card is closed.

PRESENT PERFECT

***

Pop-up boxes are particularly pleasing to make because, unlike other techniques, they fully enclose a space to create a real sense of volume. The lid pieces need to be accurately cut so that the top closes fully.

MATERIALS	SIZES
• backing sheet: thin textured grey card glued to mounting card • box and ribbons: yellow and red thick paper	backing sheet: 28 × 16 cm/ 11 × 6½ in length of box: 24 cm/9½ in (excluding tab) scale of grid: 1:2

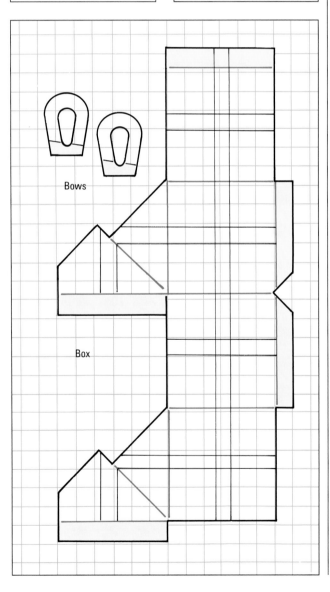

Bows

Box

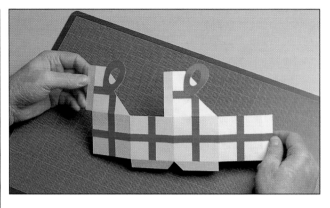

 1 *Apply glue to the underside of the bows, position on the box and glue in place. Crease as shown.*

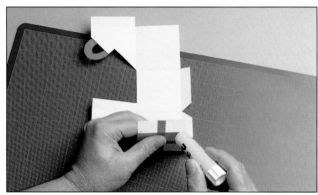

 2 *Apply glue to the end tab.*

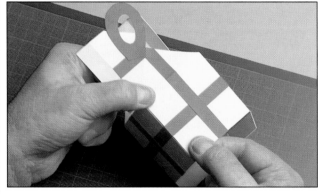

KEY

———— cut along this line

———— mountain crease

glue here (sometimes on the underside)

 3 *Make a square "tube".*

Apply glue to each lid tab in turn. The photograph shows the outer *face* of a tab being glued, so that the tab lies inside the box. However, if the inner *face* is glued, so that the tab lies outside the box, the pop-up has more strength and will not burst. The disadvantage, though, is that the tab will be seen, so decide which is best for your card.

Glue the underside of the tabs at the base of the box. Note that the tabs are folded inwards.

Glue the box to the backing sheet, using the "V" fold technique (see Getting Started, earlier).

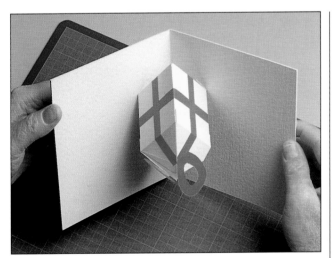

This shows how the pop-up box closes. Note how the lid pieces separate.

WHERE'S RUDOLPH?

✳✳

The crease pattern used here to make Santa Claus open out will be familiar to anyone who has made an origami Waterbomb. Indeed, many origami bases and techniques can be adapted for use in pop-up designs. A close study of the similarities between these two papercrafts can be the source of many inspiring ideas!

<table>
<tr><td>

MATERIALS

- backing sheet: blue paper glued to mounting card
- Santa: medium weight white paper
- marker pens

</td><td>

SIZES

backing sheet: 38 × 19 cm
15½ × 7½ in
height of Santa: 27 cm/
10½in
scale of grid: 1:2

</td></tr>
</table>

KEY

 cut along this line

———— suggested artwork

———— mountain crease

———— valley crease

[ ] glue here (sometimes on the underside)

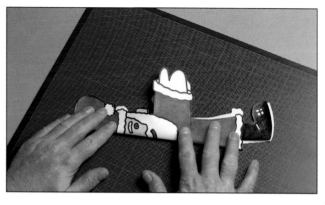

 1 *Crease down the middle, so that the artwork is on the outside of the fold. Open out.*

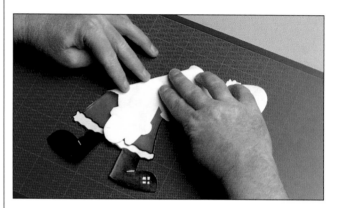

 2 *Artwork side up, crease one of the diagonals. Open out.*

 3 *Repeat, folding the other diagonal. Both diagonals need to cross the middle crease at the same point.*

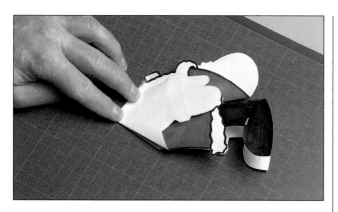

4 *Santa will collapse along the creases.*

6 *Glue the hands to the backing sheet.*

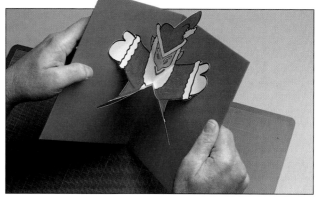

5 *Apply glue to the underside of both hands.*

7 *Note that the card will not open flat.*

FOR BEST RESULTS ...

● Place the three creases that cross Santa precisely – make a rough, undecorated Santa and experiment with the best placements of the creases before creasing your final actual figure.

DECK THE HALLS

✳✳✳✳

Chain decorations are a familiar sight at Christmas and are actually a form of pop-up design themselves! If the backing sheet on the completed greetings card is split into four sections and the creases are locked open, the card will correctly display a length of chain. Instead of making a chain, a purchased chain can be cut to length and substituted, perhaps with a more complex shape.

 1 *Bring together two chain links of different colours, fancy side out.*

 2 *Staple together just one pair of diagonally opposite corners only.*

 3 *Bring in another link of the first colour, so that its fancy side touches the fancy side of the second colour. Staple together just the second and third pieces at those diagonally opposite corners not stapled in step 2.*

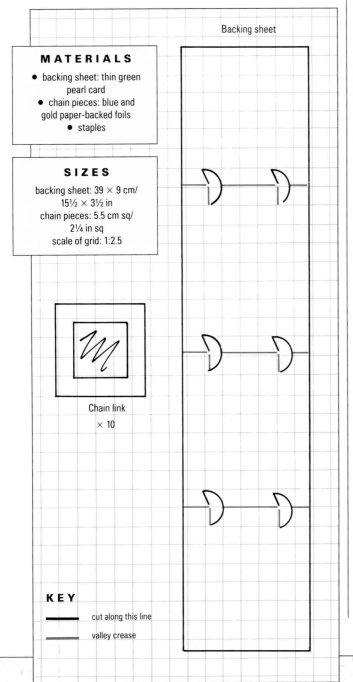

MATERIALS

- backing sheet: thin green pearl card
- chain pieces: blue and gold paper-backed foils
- staples

SIZES

backing sheet: 39 × 9 cm/
15½ × 3½ in
chain pieces: 5.5 cm sq/
2¼ in sq
scale of grid: 1:2.5

Backing sheet

Chain link
× 10

KEY

━━━━ cut along this line

──── valley crease

 4 This is the result of step 3.

 **6** Staple the end link to one end panel of the backing card.

 5

Repeat this pattern, alternating the colours so that fancy side always touches fancy side (and plain always touches plain), stapling alternate layers of diagonally opposite corners through two layers. When pulled open, this zigzag chain pattern emerges.

 7 Then staple the other end of the chain to the other end panel.

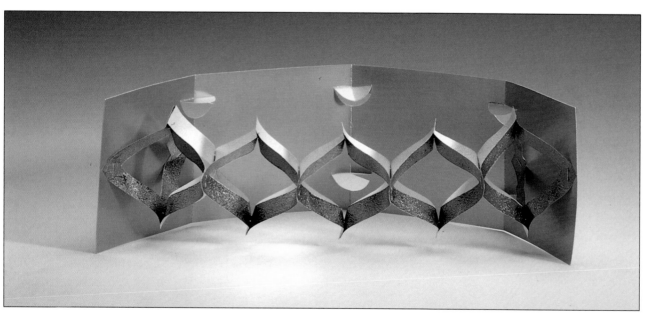

MATERIALS

- backing sheet: thin red glossy card
- letters: blue and yellow glossy card
- cracker: blue foil on white card

SIZES

backing sheet: 30 × 20 cm/ 12 × 8 in
height of letters: 7 cm/2¾ in
scale of grid: 1:2

WHAT A CRACKER!

****

Most pop-up cards open with a single crease, but here, to mimic the movement of an exploding cracker, two creases are needed. To hold the design tight shut during transit, a lock must be constructed across the central opening. Note how the four pop-up elements fly off two small rectangular tabs cut from the backing sheet and off two triangles glued to it. The triangles may be cut from the backing sheet, but this will weaken the card.

KEY

▬▬▬	cut along this line
-----	suggested artwork
▬▬▬	mountain crease
▬▬▬	valley crease
▭	glue here (sometimes on the underside)

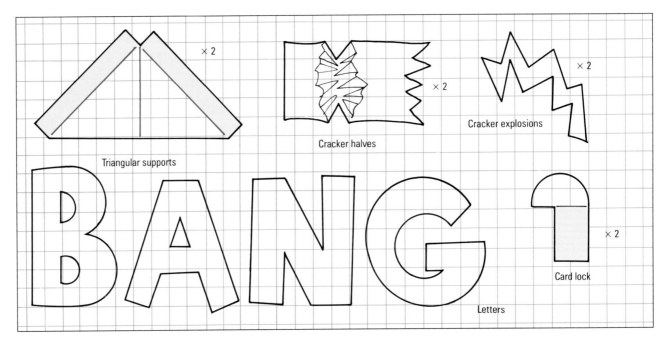

× 2

Triangular supports

Cracker halves

× 2

Cracker explosions

× 2

× 2

Card lock

Letters

BANG

Incise small square tabs as shown, one on each crease on the backing sheet. Then glue the triangular supports flat against the creases.

2 This is how you need to place the triangular supports.

3 Glue the letters "B" and "A" to the left-hand support.

4 Similarly, glue "N" and "G" to the other.

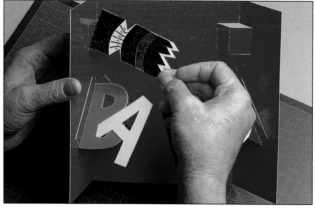

5 Glue one cracker half to the left-hand square tab.

6 Similarly, glue the other half to the right-hand square tab.

7 Add the explosions!

38

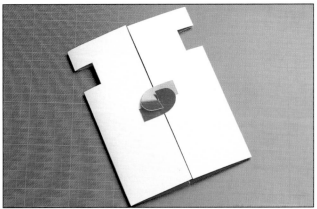

 Close the card and add the two halves of the lock, intertwining them.

 Carefully aligned, the lock halves will hold the card tightly shut.

BE CREATIVE

The two square and two triangular tabs that support the cracker halves and "BANG" can be used to support other shapes, such as Birthday names, wedding bells or a New Year message. The technique is much too versatile to confine to just this card, so let your imagination run wild and invent your own applications!

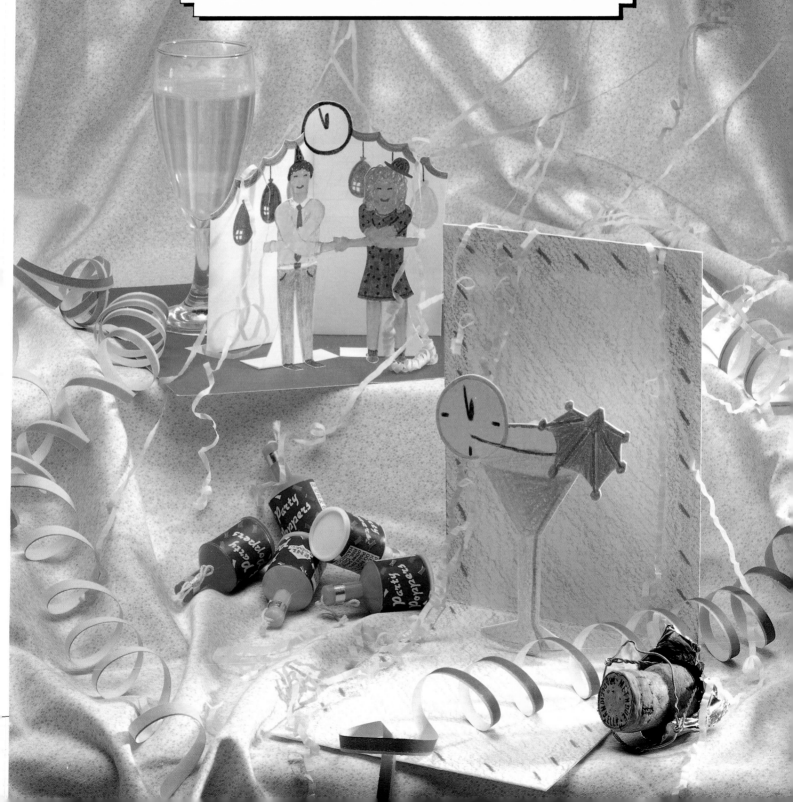

NEW YEAR

TOAST IN THE NEW YEAR

✳✳

At first glance this is a simple pop-up of a New Year cocktail. A closer look reveals the slice of lemon to be a clock face with the hands approaching midnight!

MATERIALS

- backing sheet: thick watercolour paper
- cocktail: thick watercolour paper
- coloured pencils

SIZES

backing sheet: 40 × 29 cm/
16 × 11½ in
height of cocktail: 14 cm/
5½ in
scale of grid: 1:2

KEY

——————	cut along this line
~~	suggested artwork
——————	mountain crease
——————	valley crease
▭	glue here (sometimes on the underside)

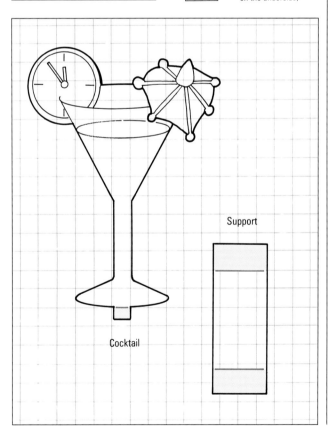

Support

Cocktail

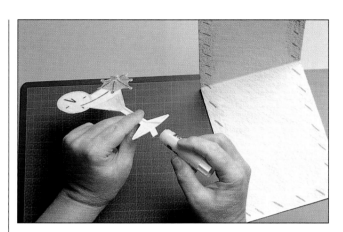

1

Apply glue to the tab at the base of the glass.

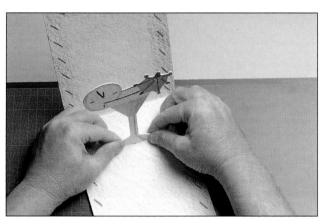

2

Glue the tab to the backing sheet.

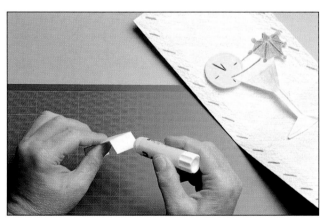

3

Apply glue to both ends of the supporting tab.

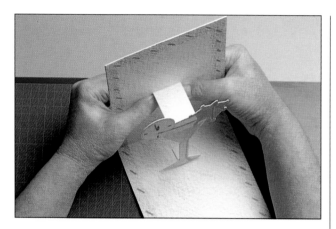

 4 Glue the tab to the glass and backing sheet, using the tab technique (see Getting Started, under Tab).

 5 The pop-up mechanism is now complete. Note the way that the glass collapses forwards when the card is shut.

48

ALL CHANGE!

✳✳✳

The movement of a trellis fence as it is pulled open is a movement that can be adapted to a pop-up greetings card and this card opens in such a way. Uniquely in the book, this pop-up design is *sewn* to the backing sheet. Using this technique, the pop-up does not erect itself along a crease (as is normally the case), but pivots open about a point.

MATERIALS

- backing sheet: thin green card glued to mounting card
- trellis pieces: yellow and pink thin card
- red and blue markers

SIZES

backing sheet: 28 × 9 cm/
11 × 3½ in
length of trellis piece: 28 cm/
11 in
scale of grid: 1:2.5

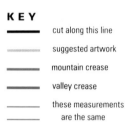

KEY

———	cut along this line
———	suggested artwork
———	mountain crease
———	valley crease
———	these measurements are the same

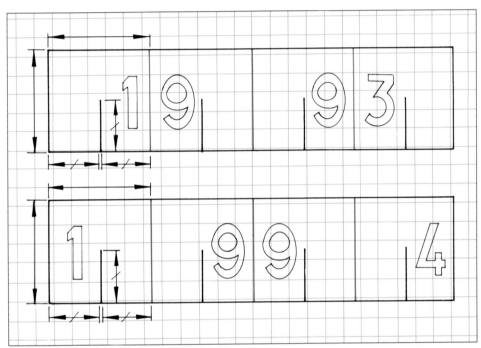

 1 Interlock the two halves by placing them in the slits.

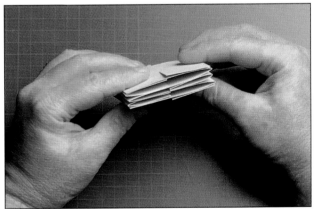

 2 Collapse the structure flat.

Tape the thread securely flat.

Lay a length of thread neatly down the middle of the end section. The right hand edge is the bottom edge of the numbers.

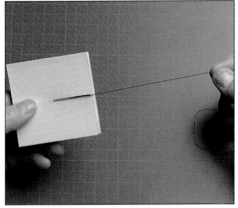

It should look like this.

Repeat steps 3–5 at the other end.

Push the needle through the backing sheet at the point at which, when the trellis is half opened (see step 12), the thread will touch the backing sheet.

Pull the thread through.

 9 *Pull it tight.*

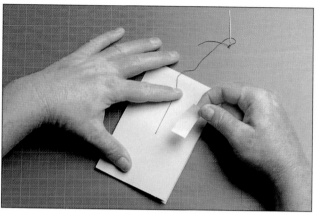

 11 *It will look like this. Repeat steps 6–9 on the other side.*

 10 *Tape the thread securely to the underside of the backing sheet.*

 12 *When the card is opened, the trellis opens with it, pulled open by the thread.*

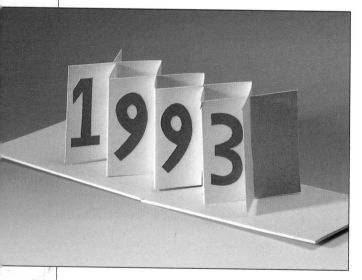

BIRTHDAYS

ANNA

FOR THE UNDER 10's

✱✱✱

Like the Time to Light the Candle card later in this chapter, the design uses a single piece of card and the same cut-away technique to make part of the pop-up stand freely (in this case, the top half of the number). When making the card, measure the distances carefully so that the number is well proportioned and placed well.

MATERIALS
- medium weight blue paper
- yellow circle stickers
- coloured pencils

SIZES
sheet size: 32 × 15 cm/
12¾ × 6 in
scale of grid: 1:2.5

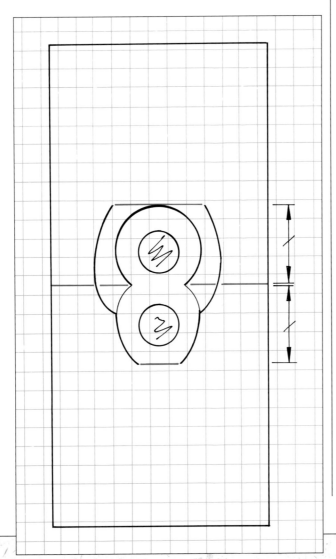

 1   Cut along the solid lines shown on the template drawing.

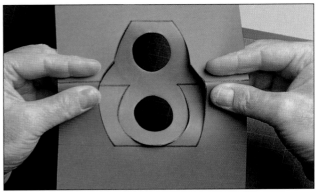

 2   Fold the two ends of the central crease.

 3   Fold the bottom crease.

KEY

▬▬▬	cut along this line
▬▬▬	suggested artwork
▬▬▬	mountain crease
▬▬▬	valley crease
▬▬▬	these measurements are the same

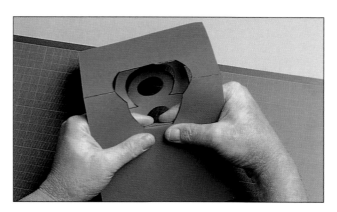

4 Then fold along the top one. Turn the card over.

5 Finally, fold the remaining short central creases each side of the number.

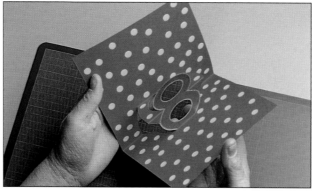

6 This is the completed pop-up shape, which will fold flat.

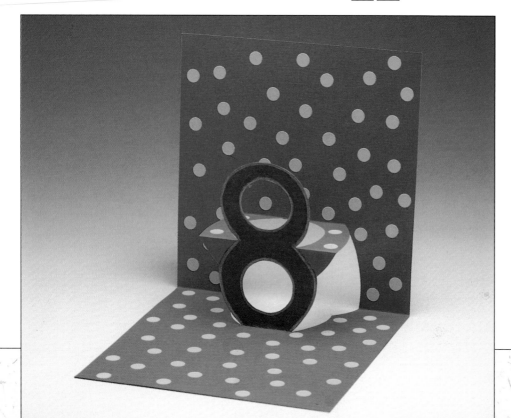

BE CREATIVE

To work out the geometry of a single-piece pop-up design such as this card is, surprisingly, something of a challenge. The simple step shape used here, with the top half of the number lifted up from it, can be adapted to any other number, letter, word or object – in fact, any silhouette is possible. Just keep those ideas coming!

COMING OF AGE

**

The X shape that connects the pop-up numbers to the backing sheet opens and closes with a scissor action that is a simplified version of the trellis action that powers the All Change! card in the previous chapter. The angle of the X can be altered if you want to present the numbers more closed up or not standing out as far from the backing sheet.

1 Slot together the two supports.

MATERIALS	SIZES
• backing sheet: pink foil glued to mounting card • supports: thick gold card • numerals: thin green card	backing sheet: 42 × 13 cm/ 16¾ × 5 in height of numerals: 11 cm/ 4½ in scale of grid: 1:2

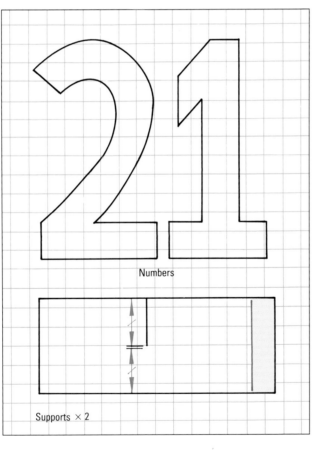

Numbers

Supports × 2

2 They will fit together like this.

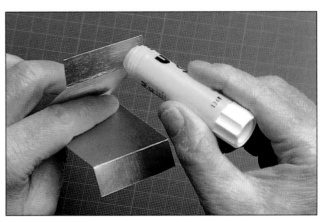

3 Apply glue to the tabs.

KEY

 cut along this line

—— mountain crease

▭ glue here (sometimes on the underside)

—— these measurements are the same

4 Glue the tabs to the backing sheet, each the same distance either side of the central crease.

6 Similarly, glue the "1" to the right-hand support.

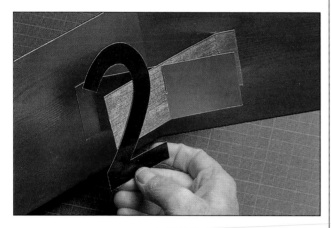

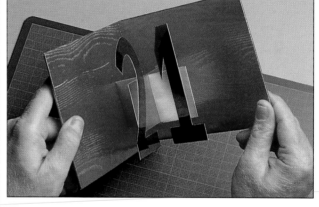

5 Glue the "2" to the left-hand support.

7 The pop-up element is now complete. Note how the supports display the numbers prominently.

56

A SLICE OF CAKE

✳✳

This design is really like half of the box used in the Present Perfect card in the Christmas chapter or a basic "V" fold with the top lidded over. Although there are seemingly many different pop-up techniques, they are often simply combinations of two or more basic techniques.

MATERIALS

- backing sheet: thick mirror card
- cake: thin white card
- felt tip pens

SIZES

backing sheet: 26 × 16 cm/
10¼ × 6½ in
length of cake crease:
11 cm/4½ in
scale of grid: 1:2

KEY

——— cut along this line

········· suggested artwork

━━━ mountain crease

━━━ valley crease

▨ glue here (sometimes on the underside)

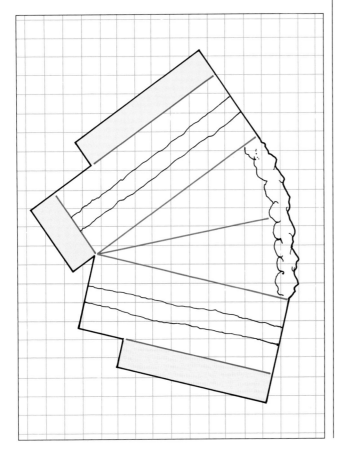

 Cut the two slits in the backing sheet.

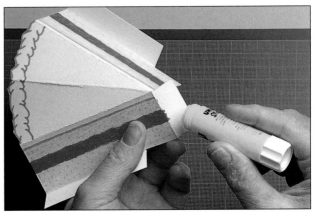

 Fold the cake along the lines and glue the tab on the point of the cake wedge to make the cake three dimensional.

 Push the tabs along the bottom of the cake through the slits.

 4 They should fit through them like this.

 5 Tape the tabs flat on the reverse of the backing sheet.

 6

The cake complete. Reflective card will make this slice of cake appear to be many!

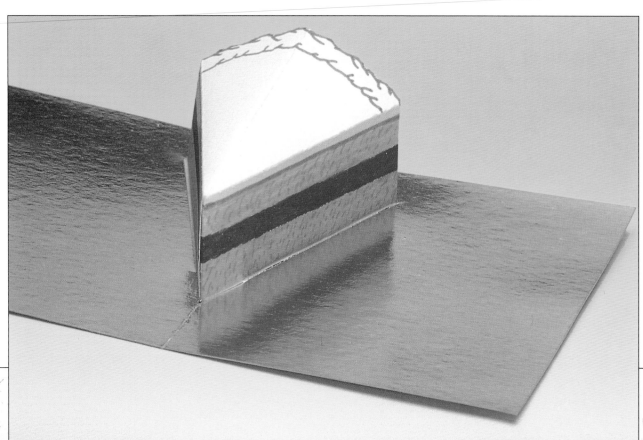

58

LIGHT THE CANDLE

✳✳

One-piece pop-ups are always satisfying to make because you see a three-dimensional shape magically emerge from what was a flat piece of card. The geometry, though, can sometimes be a little mystifying. The key is to measure the placement of all the creases carefully and to understand which distances are equal to other distances. Nothing is arbitrary.

KEY

—— cut along this line

······ suggested artwork

—— mountain crease

—— valley crease

—— these measurements are the same

MATERIALS
- thin flesh card
- coloured pencils

SIZES
sheet size: 34 × 15 cm/
13½ × 6 in
scale of grid: 1:2.5

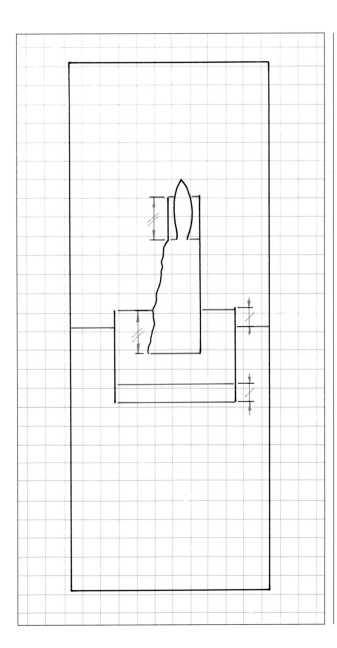

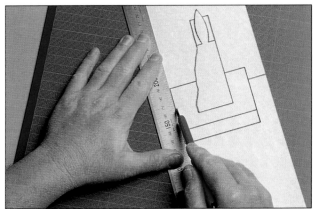

 Cut along the thick lines shown on the template drawing.

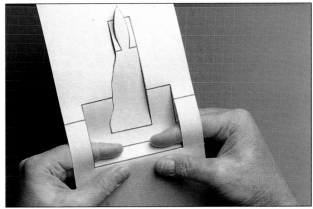

 Fold the long bottom crease.

3

Then fold the creases to each side of the candle. Turn over.

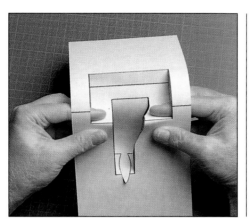

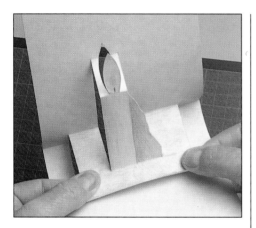

4

Fold the creases around the flame.

5   Fold the front edge of the step.

6   *The completed pop-up card. Careful measuring and creasing will permit the candle to fold flat.*

60

MATERIALS
- backing sheet: thick marbled card
- letters: thick pink card
- black marker pen

BIRTHDAY GIRL

✳✳✳

By carefully measuring and cutting, tabs of different proportions can easily be constructed. These tabs can then be used to support whatever images, words or numerals are appropriate.

SIZES
backing sheet: 30 × 21 cm/
12 × 8½ in
height of letters: 5 cm/2 in
scale of grid: 1:2.5

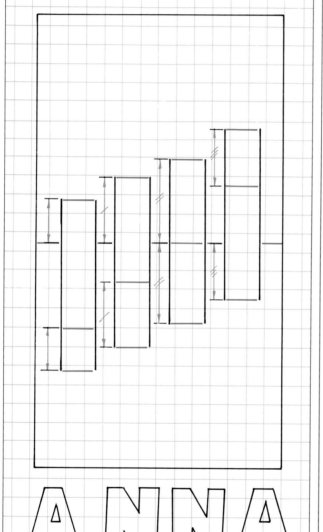

Cut the slits as indicated on the template drawing.

Form the short, horizontal creases.

Carefully fold the card in half, forming all the creases simultaneously.

KEY

▬▬ cut along this line	▬▬ valley crease
▬▬ mountain crease	▬▬ these measurements are the same

4   *Open the card and you will find that the folded strips form steps.*

6   *Continue in the same way, from left to right, until you have completed the name.*

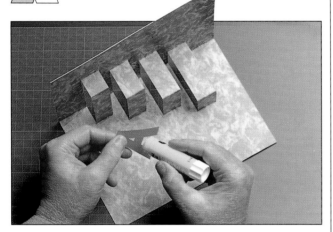

5   *Glue the first letter to the left-hand step.*

7   *Magically, the addition of the letters will not prevent the card from being closed.*

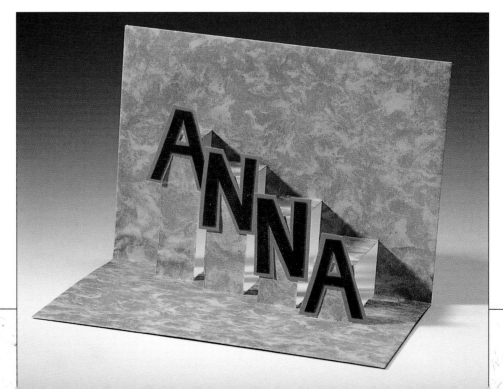

62

BIRTHDAY BOY

**

The key to successful pop-up cards is the careful use of angles. In this design, the angles of the tab that connect the name to the backing sheet are important, because they must present the name in the best way – neither too horizontal nor too vertical. Cut the support with care and glue it to the backing sheet at the correct angle.

MATERIALS
- backing sheet: thick green paper glued to mounting card
- support: thick green paper
- letters: light green thick paper
- silver foil

SIZES
backing sheet: 38 × 14 cm/
15¼ × 5½ in
width of support: 20 cm/8 in
scale of grid: 1:2.5

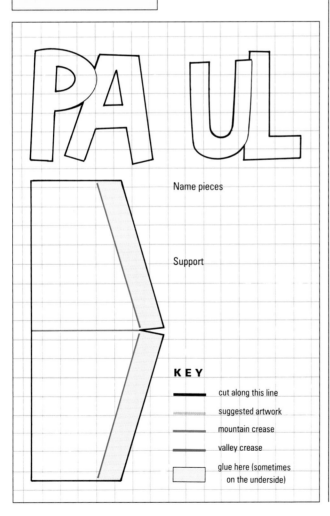

Name pieces

Support

KEY

────── cut along this line

────── suggested artwork

────── mountain crease

────── valley crease

▭ glue here (sometimes on the underside)

1 *Apply glue to the letters "PA". Glue them to the left-hand side of the support. Glue the letters "UL" to the right-hand side.*

2 *Apply glue to the base of the support where shown on the template.*

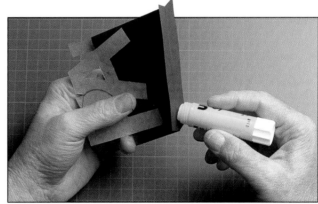

3 *Glue the support to the backing sheet, using the "V" fold technique (see Getting Started under "V" fold).*

GIFT TOKEN

✱✱✱✱

At some time or another you are likely to want to give someone a gift token, cash or cheque for their birthday, Christmas or whenever. Simply handing it to them in an envelope hardly celebrates the occasion, so this pop-up card provides you with a stylish alternative. The hand holds a small envelope that contains the gift, which pops forward in a gesture of giving as the card is opened!

MATERIALS

- backing sheet: thick mottled beige paper glued to mounting card
- supports: thick mottled beige paper
- white, brown and black card

SIZES

backing sheet: 20 × 20 cm/
8 × 8 in
length of hand and sleeve:
13 cm/5 in
scale of grid: 1:2.5

KEY

▬▬▬	cut along this line
▬▬▬	suggested artwork
▬▬▬	mountain crease
▬▬▬	valley crease
▭	glue here (sometimes on the underside)
▬ ▬	these measurements are the same

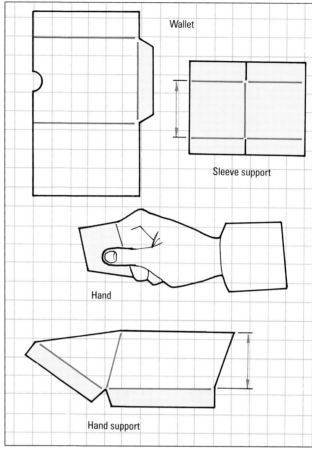

Wallet

Sleeve support

Hand

Hand support

1

Apply glue to the side of the wallet piece.

2

Apply it, too, along the bottom and fold it together to create the completed wallet.

CONGRATULATIONS

✱✱✱

At first sight, this spectacular design may look extremely difficult. However, it is made using a single, simple technique, based on dividing the card in half, then quarters, then eighths, then sixteenths. With a little practice, the card can be made in just a few minutes, honestly!

MATERIALS	SIZES
• medium weight orange paper • dark felt tin pen	sheet size: 16 × 17 cm/ 6½ × 6¾ in scale of grid: 1:2.5

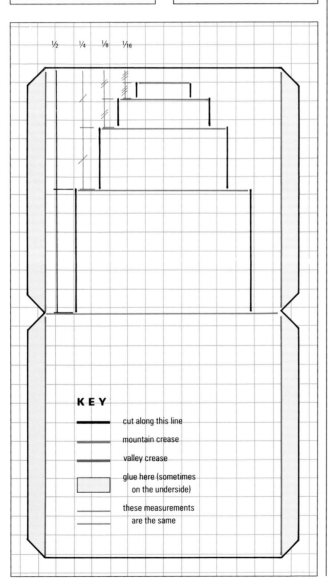

½ ¼ ⅛ ¹⁄₁₆

KEY

— cut along this line

— mountain crease

— valley crease

⬜ glue here (sometimes on the underside)

— these measurements are the same

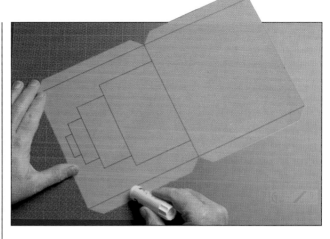

Apply glue to the four long edge tabs.

Fold the centre crease and keep it closed.

Cut the first pair of long slits – the long ones.

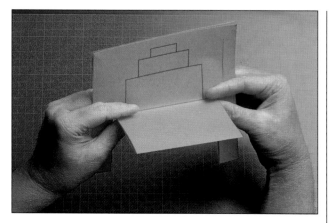

 4 Crease between the ends of the cuts.

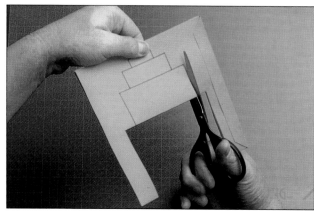

7 Cut along the next pair of medium-length slits, now cutting through four layers.

5 Open the card and lift this central section out of the middle. Re-crease the central valley crease as a mountain.

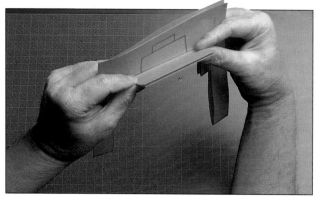

8 Crease between the ends of the cuts.

6 This creates a step. Fold the card shut to encase the step.

9 As before, pull the cut sections up into the card and re-crease to form two steps, one each side of the centre.

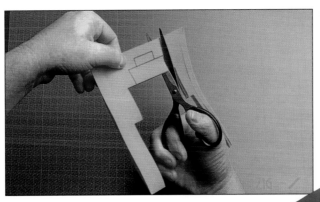

 10

Repeat with the next pair of slits, first cutting. Then folding as before.

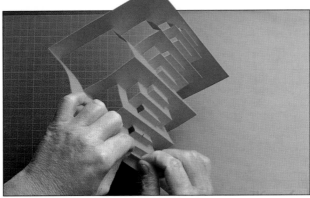

 11

This will create four steps.

 12

Finally, repeat the cut, fold and pull sequence with the final drawn lines at the very top of the card, to create eight new steps. Now write "Congratulations" on the card.

VALENTINE'S DAY

CUPID'S ARROW

**

There is a certain elegance when a supporting tab becomes part of the design. In this case, the tab that supports the heart has become the arrow. Thus, no part of the design is superfluous. Note also how the arrow slides through the heart when the card is opened – very dramatic.

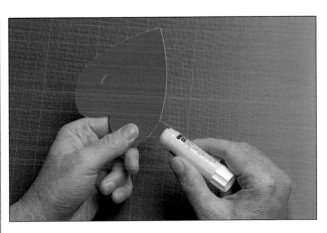

MATERIALS	SIZES
• backing sheet: thin glossy yellow card • heart and arrow: red and blue thin card	backing sheet: 35 × 11 cm/ 14 × 4½ in height of heart: 10.5 cm/ 4½ in scale of grid: 1:2

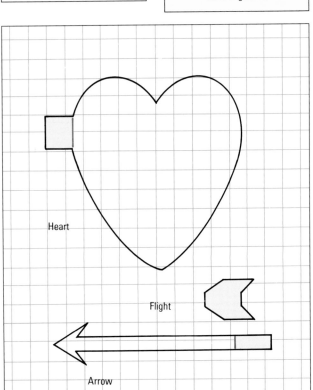

Heart

Flight

Arrow

KEY

———— cut along this line

---------- suggested artwork

———— mountain crease

———— valley crease

[ ] glue here (sometimes on the underside)

1 Apply glue to the heart tab.

2 Glue the tab to the backing sheet, so that the crease on the backing sheet lies approximately behind the centre line of the heart.

3 Feed the arrow through the slit in the heart from right to left.

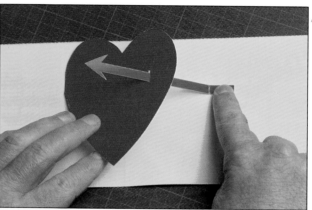

 4 *Glue it to the backing sheet.*

 5 *Glue the flight to the end of the arrow.*

BE CREATIVE

The technique of piercing one pop-up shape with another need not be confined to a large shape (the heart) pierced by a thin one (the arrow). Any shape can pierce any other, eliminating the need – as here – for extra supporting tabs.

SAY IT WITH FLOWERS

✳✳

MATERIALS

- backing sheet: white mounting card
- flowers and vase: thick watercolour paper
- felt tip pens

This is a simple design in technical terms, but it is perhaps the most decoratively versatile design in the book. The specific shapes of vase, foliage and blooms are only a suggestion – try roses, tulips or, more personal, your loved one's favourite flowers.

SIZES

backing sheet: 48 × 23 cm/ 19 × 9 in
height of back layer of flowers: 20 cm/8 in
scale of grid: 1:2.5

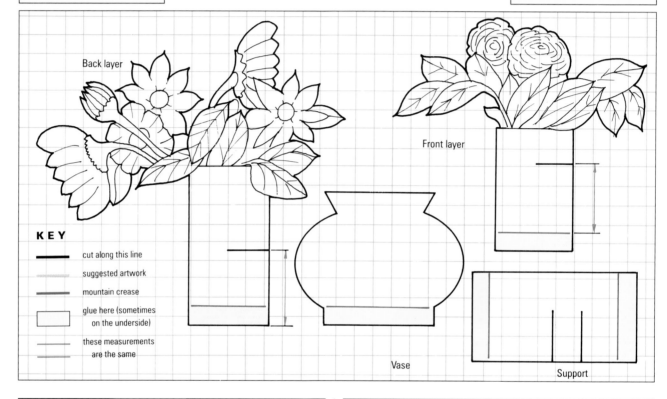

Back layer

Front layer

KEY

——— cut along this line

——— suggested artwork

——— mountain crease

▭ glue here (sometimes on the underside)

—— these measurements are the same

Vase

Support

1   *Apply glue to the right-hand edge of the support.*

2   *Glue it horizontally to the backing sheet.*

Apply glue to the base of the back layer of flowers.

Slot it into the first slit in the support (that nearest the backing sheet) and fix the tab to the backing sheet. (This assembly uses the tab technique – (see Getting Started under Tab).

Repeat steps 3 and 4 for the front layer of flowers.

Glue the vase to the front of the support to complete the pop-up structure.

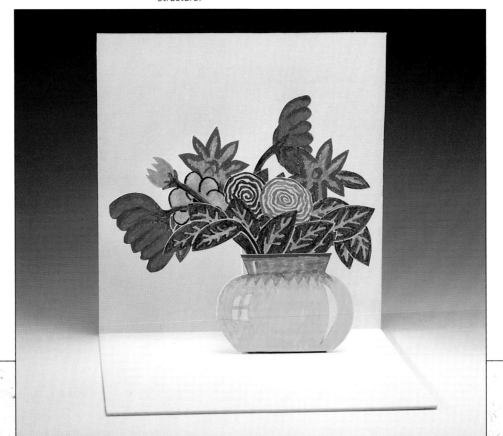

TRUE LOVE

*

This is perhaps the simplest pop-up design in the book. Note how the card is folded behind to create a double thickness that prevents the design from buckling. This also means that the design can be made from paper, rather than card.

MATERIALS
- medium weight red paper

SIZES
sheet size: 20 × 26 cm/
8 × 10¼ in (fully opened)
scale of grid: 1:2.5

KEY
——— cut along this line
——— mountain crease
——— valley crease

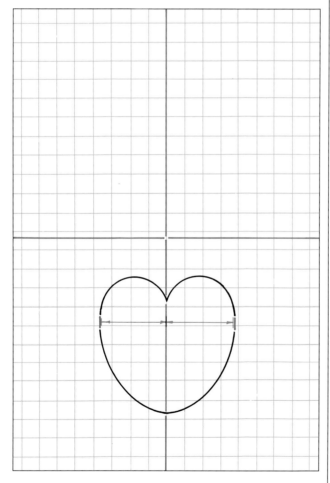

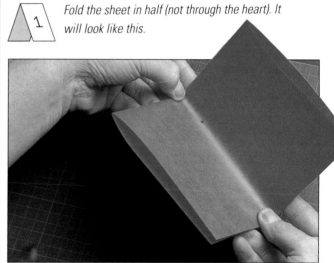

 Fold the sheet in half (not through the heart). It will look like this.

Then fold in half again. It will now look like this.

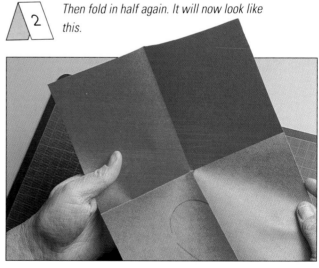

Open the sheet out. Note the position of the half-heart drawing.

Cut out the heart, being careful to leave the small sections uncut that are marked to be creased on the template.

Fold back the heart to create these creases.

This is the completed card. Note the crease formation around the heart.

Re-form the folds and pull up the heart, creating a mountain fold down the centre of the heart.

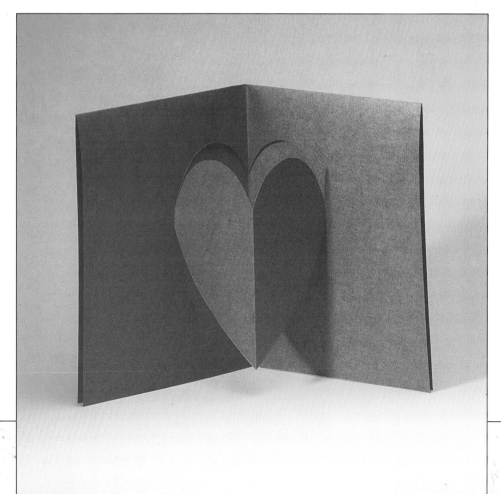

78

LONELY HEART

✳✳

If you think the other single heart design was a quiet one, this one is much more exuberant – the heart rises away from the backing sheet when the card is opened. The design can also be made from a single sheet, though it will not be quite so robust.

MATERIALS
- backing sheet and heart: thick textured watercolour paper
- coloured pencils

SIZES
backing sheet: 29 × 9 cm/ 11½ × 3½ in
height of heart: 13 cm/5 in
scale of grid: 1:2

KEY

———— cut along this line

———— mountain crease

———— valley crease

[☐] glue here (sometimes on the underside)

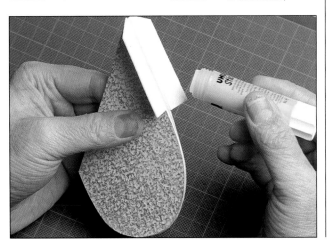

 Apply glue to the tabs at the base of the heart.

 Glue the tabs to the backing sheet, using the "V" fold technique (see Getting Started).

 The completed card. Note the width of the backing sheet, needed to accommodate the height of the heart when the card is shut.

KISS ME QUICK

✳✳✳✳✳

This passionate design will work only if the placement of the two heads is carefully measured – otherwise the kissers will miss their targets! Note how differently the supports for each head are made. To simplify the design, both heads could be made using the same technique, though they would not then be on different planes.

MATERIALS

- backing sheet: thick maroon paper glued to mounting card
- supports: same paper
- head and heart: textured white thin card
- coloured pencils

SIZES

backing sheet: 32 × 26 cm/ 12¾ × 10¼ in
height of heads: 12 cm/4¾ in
scale of grid: 1:2.5

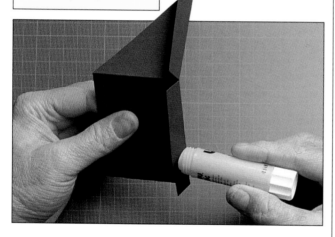

 1 Apply glue to the tabs of the main support for him.

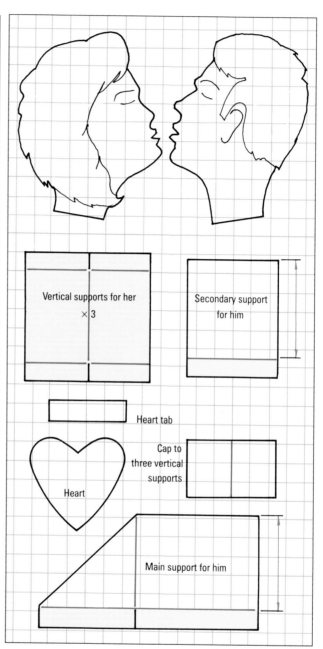

Vertical supports for her × 3

Secondary support for him

Heart tab

Heart

Cap to three vertical supports

Main support for him

 2

Glue it to the backing sheet, using the "V" fold technique (see Getting Started under "V" fold).

KEY

▬▬▬	cut along this line
┄┄┄	suggested artwork
▬▬▬	mountain crease
▬▬▬	valley crease
▭	glue here (sometimes on the underside)
────	these measurements are the same

 Add the secondary support, parallel to it.

 Stick tape along the tops of both these supports (the head may need to be moved in step 15).

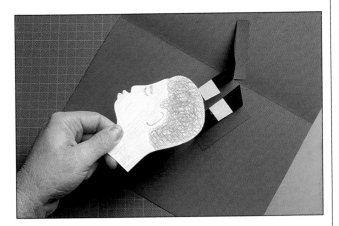

 Fix the man's head to the supports.

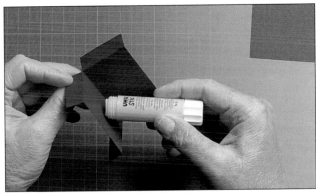

 Apply glue to the inside of one of the vertical supports for her, between the creases at each end.

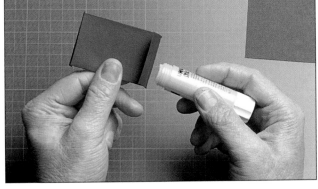

 Fold it in half, fold back the two tabs at one end and apply glue to them.

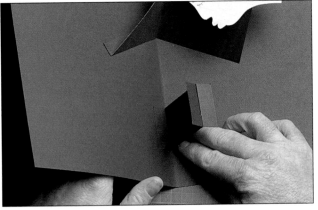

 Fix those glued tabs to each side of the central crease on the backing sheet.

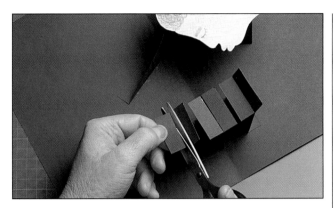

9 Repeat with the remaining two vertical supports. Glue one to each side of the central vertical support. Trim off the extreme left-hand tab.

12 Glue on the heart tab.

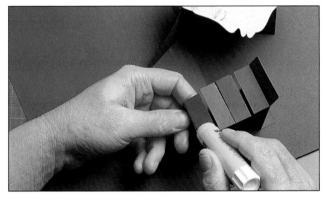

10 Glue the remaining five tabs.

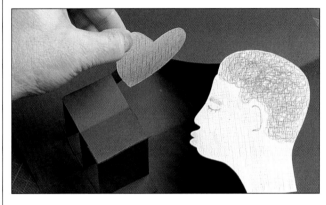

13 Glue the heart to the tab.

11 Carefully press in place the cap to the vertical supports.

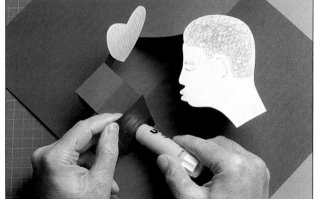

14 Apply glue to the front vertical support.

Fix her head to the support, positioning it so that the two mouths meet. If his head is in the wrong place, adjust it as necessary.

 The completed pop-up design, with the mouths meeting!

 When the card is shut, his head swivels away to the right.

HALLOWE'EN

98

RAINING CONFETTI

✳✳✳

MATERIALS
- backing sheet: thick mottled grey card
- hand and confetti box: thick watercolour paper
- confetti
- felt tip pens

This pop-up design is a pleasant change from the usual designs for weddings. When it is being opened, the hand swivels downwards, mimicking the action of showering the happy couple with confetti. Note that when the card is flat, the hand extends beyond the backing sheet.

SIZES
backing sheet: 30 × 25 cm/ 12 × 10 in
length of hand: 12 cm/4¾ in
scale of grid: 1:2.5

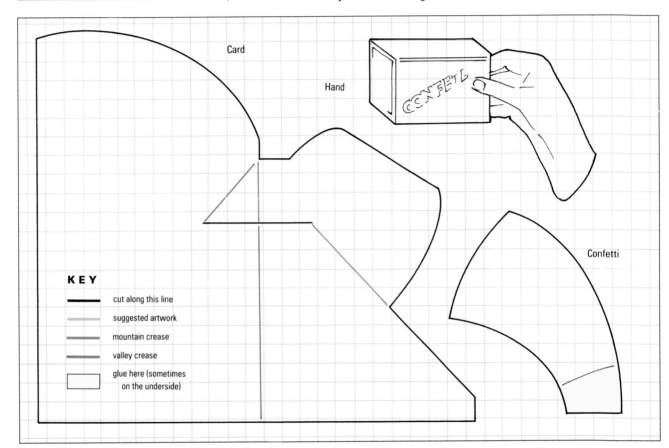

Card

Hand

Confetti

KEY

———	cut along this line
———	suggested artwork
———	mountain crease
———	valley crease
▭	glue here (sometimes on the underside)

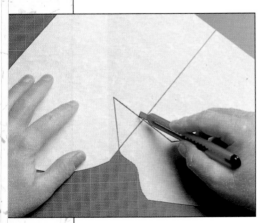

 1

Cut the backing sheet as indicated by the template drawing.

 2

Make the long central creases.

 3 *Make the smaller folds.*

 6 *Your card will now look like this. Adjust the angle of the hand if it does not swivel effectively when the card is opened.*

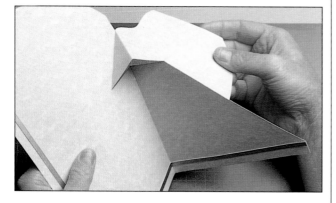

 4 *You will now have this shape, which will also fold flat again.*

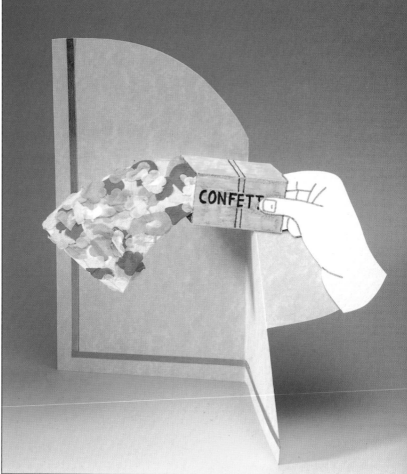

 5 *Fix the hand and confetti pieces to the supporting shelf, passing the confetti pieces through the slot in the confetti box.*

MATERIALS

- backing sheet: thin blue card glued to mounting card
- mechanism pieces: thin blue card
- ring: gold foil card

SIZES

backing sheet: 34 × 15 cm/ 13½ × 6 in
length of ring: 16 cm/6½ in (excluding tab)
scale of grid: 1:2.5

A WEDDING RING

✳✳✳

Like the Witch's Hat card earlier in the Hallowe'en chapter, this unusual pop-up design creates a curved form when the card is opened. The technique can be adapted to create any curved form, such as a face, an Easter egg or shirt sleeve. The mechanics of the pop-up will be visible, though, unless they and the backing sheet are constructed from dark card that will absorb shadows. Here a paler colour of card has been used so that you can see clearly how the pieces fit together.

KEY

——— cut along this line

——— mountain crease

——— valley crease

⬜ glue here (sometimes on the underside)

——— these measurements are the same

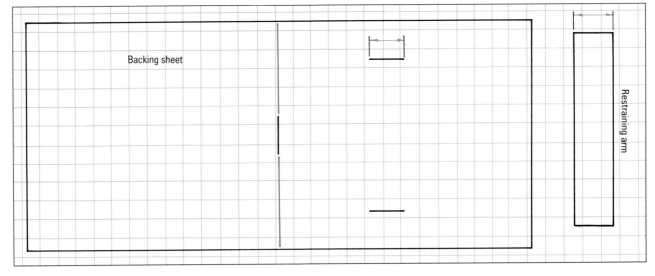

Backing sheet

Restraining arm

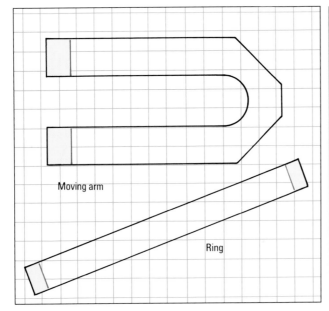

Moving arm

Ring

 1

Cut the two short slits in the backing sheet.

Similarly, cut the short central slit.

Apply glue to the moving arm tabs.

Glue the moving arm to the backing sheet as shown. Note that the tabs lie to the left of the central crease.

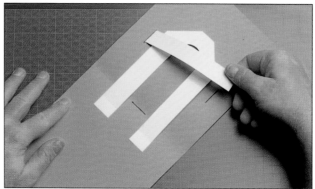

Push the restraining arm through one slit.

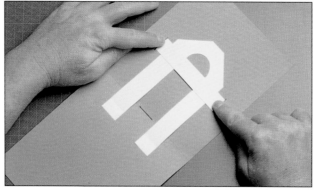

Then push it through the other. Secure each end on the reverse of the backing sheet with glue or tape.

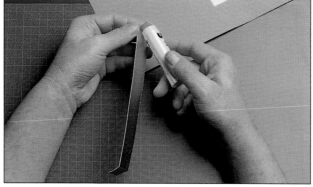

Apply glue to the inside of each tab at the ends of the ring strip.

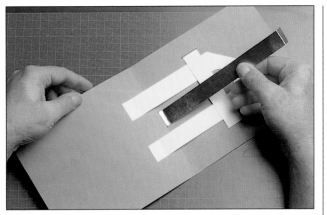

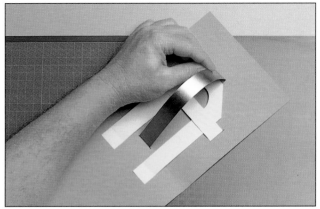

 Push one tab through the central slit and glue securely behind.

 Glue the other tab to the top of the moving arm. The ring will now curve.

BE CREATIVE

A wedding ring is a plain band, but an engagement ring is a more complicated shape. The pop-up design shown here can easily be adapted, though, to depict an engagement ring. Use coloured foils to capture the sparkle of the gem stones.

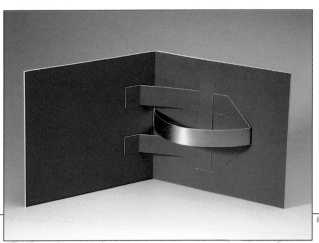

 10

As the card is closed, the ring will flatten.

MOVING HOUSE

MATERIALS

- backing sheet: thin pink card glued to mounting card
- van: thin green card
- felt tip pens

SIZES

backing sheet: 22 × 16 cm/
8¾ × 6½ in
length of side of van: 9.5 cm/
3¾ in (including cab)
scale of grid: 1:2

FUN REMOVALS

✳✳✳

The van in this design is a modified box, but, unlike the Present Perfect card earlier, this pop-up element lies parallel to the backing sheet, not at an angle. Using this very adaptable technique, a whole fleet of vehicles could be constructed, as well as boats, ships and aeroplanes. The sides of the van can be livened up by adding a suitably humorous removal company name that relates to the person moving house!

KEY

———	cut along this line
········	suggested artwork
———	mountain crease
———	valley crease
▭	glue here (sometimes on the underside)
———	these measurements are the same

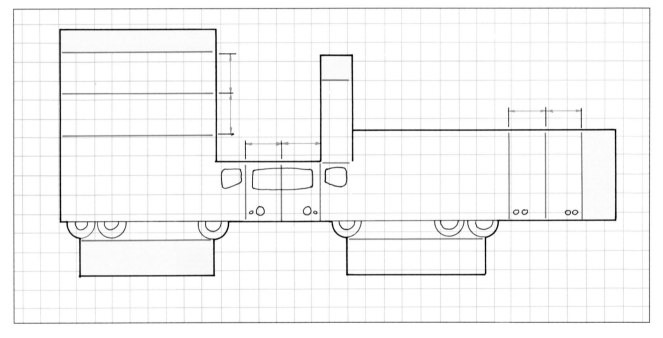

Make all the creases.

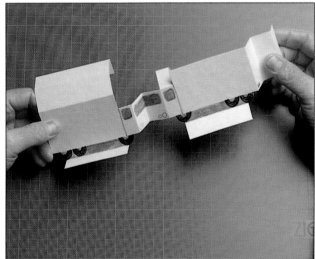

2

Apply glue to the end tab and glue it into the vehicle.

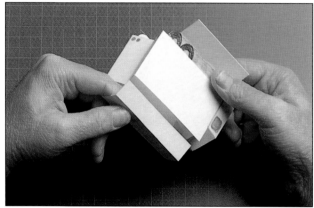

3

Glue in the two top tabs.

4

Make the slits in the backing sheet. The distance between them is the width of the vehicle.

5

Push the tabs through the slits.

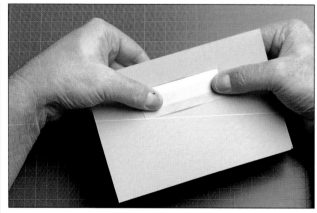

6

Tape the tabs flat to the reverse of the backing sheet.

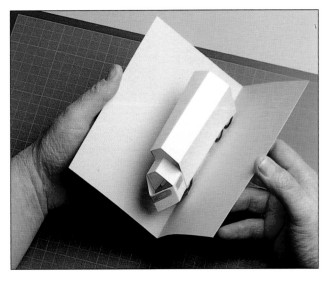

7 Note how the vehicle opens and flattens when the card is folded shut.

NEW HOME, SWEET HOME *****

This is the most complicated design in the book, but looks so good you really must try it. The house is made in a similar way to the removal van of the previous card, as is the fence, believe it or not! The "V" fold tree is attached to the backing sheet by means of a strap. The telegraph pole is attached to the fence using the tab technique, which you have employed many times already. Note the chimney. It is not attached to the roof, as you would expect, but to the backing sheet to give a three-dimensional effect.

KEY

——— cut along this line

——— suggested artwork

——— mountain crease

——— valley crease

▭ glue here (sometimes on the underside)

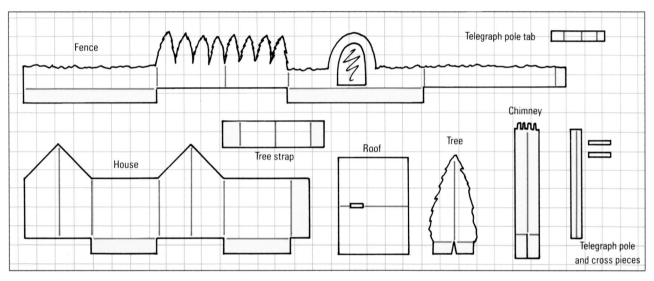

Fence

Telegraph pole tab

Chimney

Tree strap

Roof

Tree

House

Telegraph pole and cross pieces

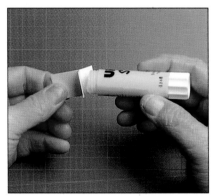

 Apply glue to both tabs on the tree strap.

 Glue the strap across the central crease on the backing sheet.

 The strap folds up when the card is closed.

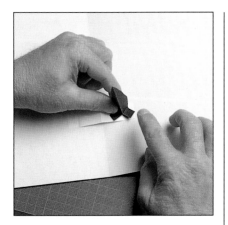

 Glue the tree to one end of the strap, using the "V" fold technique (see Getting Started under "V" fold).

 Glue the tab at the end of the house to the other end to make it three dimensional.

 Fix it in place so that it looks like this. It may take several attempts to lower it into the correct position (open out the house to check that you've got it right).

 Glue and fold the chimney so that it is double thickness and glue its tabs to the backing sheet, each side of the central crease.

 Fix masking tape to the long top edges of the house, then lower on the roof.

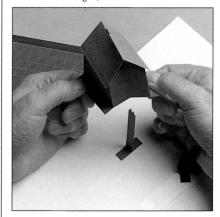

 Apply glue to the underside of the house tabs.

 Glue them to the backing sheet. Be careful not to lower the house over the chimney and to pull the house fully open.

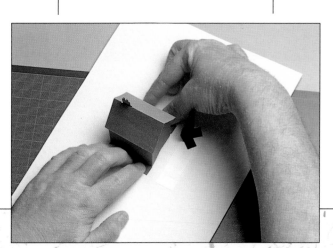

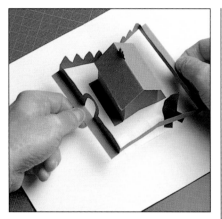

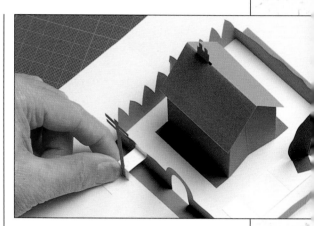

 11   In a similar way, fold and glue the fence to the backing sheet.

12   It should look like this. Stretch it so that it is square.

 13   Glue the telegraph pole tab to the fence and backing sheet. Assemble the telegraph pole and cross pieces and glue to the front of the tab.

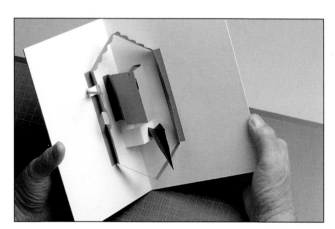

 14

This is the completed card. Note how the different pieces collapse as the card closes.

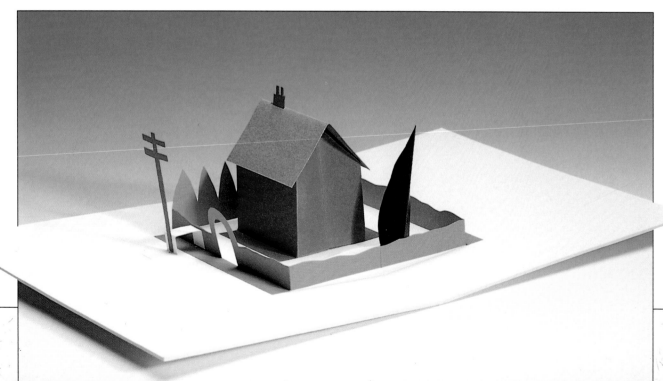